MONTHLY PLANNER 2025-2026

2025

January

Su	Mo	Tu	We	Th	Fr	Sa
			1	2	3	4
5	6	7	8	9	10	11
12	13	14	15	16	17	18
19	20	21	22	23	24	25
26	27	28	29	30	31	

February

Su	Mo	Tu	We	Th	Fr	Sa
						1
2	3	4	5	6	7	8
9	10	11	12	13	14	15
16	17	18	19	20	21	22
23	24	25	26	27	28	

March

Su	Mo	Tu	We	Th	Fr	Sa
						1
2	3	4	5	6	7	8
9	10	11	12	13	14	15
16	17	18	19	20	21	22
23	24	25	26	27	28	29
30	31					

April

Su	Mo	Tu	We	Th	Fr	Sa
		1	2	3	4	5
6	7	8	9	10	11	12
13	14	15	16	17	18	19
20	21	22	23	24	25	26
27	28	29	30			

May

Su	Mo	Tu	We	Th	Fr	Sa
				1	2	3
4	5	6	7	8	9	10
11	12	13	14	15	16	17
18	19	20	21	22	23	24
25	26	27	28	29	30	31

June

Su	Mo	Tu	We	Th	Fr	Sa
1	2	3	4	5	6	7
8	9	10	11	12	13	14
15	16	17	18	19	20	21
22	23	24	25	26	27	28
29	30					

July

Su	Mo	Tu	We	Th	Fr	Sa
		1	2	3	4	5
6	7	8	9	10	11	12
13	14	15	16	17	18	19
20	21	22	23	24	25	26
27	28	29	30	31		

August

Su	Mo	Tu	We	Th	Fr	Sa
					1	2
3	4	5	6	7	8	9
10	11	12	13	14	15	16
17	18	19	20	21	22	23
24	25	26	27	28	29	30
31						

September

Su	Mo	Tu	We	Th	Fr	Sa
	1	2	3	4	5	6
7	8	9	10	11	12	13
14	15	16	17	18	19	20
21	22	23	24	25	26	27
28	29	30				

October

Su	Mo	Tu	We	Th	Fr	Sa
			1	2	3	4
5	6	7	8	9	10	11
12	13	14	15	16	17	18
19	20	21	22	23	24	25
26	27	28	29	30	31	

November

Su	Mo	Tu	We	Th	Fr	Sa
						1
2	3	4	5	6	7	8
9	10	11	12	13	14	15
16	17	18	19	20	21	22
23	24	25	26	27	28	29
30						

December

Su	Mo	Tu	We	Th	Fr	Sa
	1	2	3	4	5	6
7	8	9	10	11	12	13
14	15	16	17	18	19	20
21	22	23	24	25	26	27
28	29	30	31			

2026

January

Su	Mo	Tu	We	Th	Fr	Sa
				1	2	3
4	5	6	7	8	9	10
11	12	13	14	15	16	17
18	19	20	21	22	23	24
25	26	27	28	29	30	31

February

Su	Mo	Tu	We	Th	Fr	Sa
1	2	3	4	5	6	7
8	9	10	11	12	13	14
15	16	17	18	19	20	21
22	23	24	25	26	27	28

March

Su	Mo	Tu	We	Th	Fr	Sa
1	2	3	4	5	6	7
8	9	10	11	12	13	14
15	16	17	18	19	20	21
22	23	24	25	26	27	28
29	30	31				

April

Su	Mo	Tu	We	Th	Fr	Sa
			1	2	3	4
5	6	7	8	9	10	11
12	13	14	15	16	17	18
19	20	21	22	23	24	25
26	27	28	29	30		

May

Su	Mo	Tu	We	Th	Fr	Sa
					1	2
3	4	5	6	7	8	9
10	11	12	13	14	15	16
17	18	19	20	21	22	23
24	25	26	27	28	29	30
31						

June

Su	Mo	Tu	We	Th	Fr	Sa
	1	2	3	4	5	6
7	8	9	10	11	12	13
14	15	16	17	18	19	20
21	22	23	24	25	26	27
28	29	30				

July

Su	Mo	Tu	We	Th	Fr	Sa
			1	2	3	4
5	6	7	8	9	10	11
12	13	14	15	16	17	18
19	20	21	22	23	24	25
26	27	28	29	30	31	

August

Su	Mo	Tu	We	Th	Fr	Sa
						1
2	3	4	5	6	7	8
9	10	11	12	13	14	15
16	17	18	19	20	21	22
23	24	25	26	27	28	29
30	31					

September

Su	Mo	Tu	We	Th	Fr	Sa
		1	2	3	4	5
6	7	8	9	10	11	12
13	14	15	16	17	18	19
20	21	22	23	24	25	26
27	28	29	30			

October

Su	Mo	Tu	We	Th	Fr	Sa
				1	2	3
4	5	6	7	8	9	10
11	12	13	14	15	16	17
18	19	20	21	22	23	24
25	26	27	28	29	30	31

November

Su	Mo	Tu	We	Th	Fr	Sa
1	2	3	4	5	6	7
8	9	10	11	12	13	14
15	16	17	18	19	20	21
22	23	24	25	26	27	28
29	30					

December

Su	Mo	Tu	We	Th	Fr	Sa
		1	2	3	4	5
6	7	8	9	10	11	12
13	14	15	16	17	18	19
20	21	22	23	24	25	26
27	28	29	30	31		

NOTES

NOTES

NOTES

IMPORTANT DATES
2025

January

February

March

April

May

June

July

August

September

October

November

December

IMPORTANT DATES
2026

January	February	March

April	May	June

July	August	September

October	November	December

JANUARY
2025

MONDAY	TUESDAY	WEDNESDAY	THURSDAY
		1	2
6	7	8	9
13	14	15	16
20	21	22	23
27	28	29	30

FRIDAY	SATURDAY	SUNDAY	NOTES
3	4	5	
10	11	12	
17	18	19	
24	25	26	
31			

FEBRUARY
2025

MONDAY	TUESDAY	WEDNESDAY	THURSDAY
3	4	5	6
10	11	12	13
17	18	19	20
24	25	26	27

FRIDAY	SATURDAY	SUNDAY	NOTES
	1	2	
7	8	9	
14	15	16	
Valentine's Day			
21	22	23	
28			

MARCH

2025

MONDAY	TUESDAY	WEDNESDAY	THURSDAY
3	4	5	6
10	11	12	13
17	18	19	20
S. 31	24	25	26	27

FRIDAY	SATURDAY	SUNDAY	NOTES
	1	2	
7	8	9	
14	15	16	
21	22	23	
28	29	30	

APRIL

2025

MONDAY	TUESDAY	WEDNESDAY	THURSDAY
	1	2	3
7	8	9	10
14	15	16	17
21	22	23	24
28	29	30	1

FRIDAY	SATURDAY	SUNDAY
4	5	6
11	12	13
18	19	20
25	26	27

MAY

2025

MONDAY	TUESDAY	WEDNESDAY	THURSDAY
			1
5	6	7	8
12	13	14	15
19	20	21	22
26	27	28	29

FRIDAY	SATURDAY	SUNDAY	NOTES
2	3	4	
9	10	11 Mother's Day	
16	17	18	
23	24	25	
30	31	1	

JUNE
2025

MONDAY	TUESDAY	WEDNESDAY	THURSDAY
2	3	4	5
9	10	11	12
16	17	18	19
23	24	25	26

FRIDAY	SATURDAY	SUNDAY	NOTES
6	7	8	
13	14 Flag Day	15 Father's Day	
20	21	22	
27	28	29	

JULY

2025

MONDAY	TUESDAY	WEDNESDAY	THURSDAY
	1	2	3
7	8	9	10
14	15	16	17
21	22	23	24
28	29	30	31

FRIDAY	SATURDAY	SUNDAY	NOTES
4 Independence Day	5	6	
11	12	13	
18	19	20	
25	26	27	

AUGUST
2025

MONDAY	TUESDAY	WEDNESDAY	THURSDAY
4	5	6	7
11	12	13	14
18	19	20	21
25	26	27	28

FRIDAY	SATURDAY	SUNDAY	NOTES
1	2	3	
8	9	10	
15	16	17	
22	23	24	
29	30	31	

SEPTEMBER

2025

MONDAY	TUESDAY	WEDNESDAY	THURSDAY
1	2	3	4
8	9	10	11
15	16	17	18
22	23	24	25
29	30		

FRIDAY	SATURDAY	SUNDAY	NOTES
5	6	7	
12	13	14	
19	20	21	
26	27	28	

OCTOBER

2025

MONDAY	TUESDAY	WEDNESDAY	THURSDAY
		1	2
6	7	8	9
13	14	15	16
20	21	22	23
27	28	29	30

FRIDAY	SATURDAY	SUNDAY	NOTES
3	4	5	
10	11	12	
17	18	19	
24	25	26	
31 Halloween			

NOVEMBER
2025

MONDAY	TUESDAY	WEDNESDAY	THURSDAY
3	4	5	6
10	11	12	13
17	18	19	20
24	25	26	27

FRIDAY	SATURDAY	SUNDAY	NOTES
	1	2	
7 'Veterans Day' day off	8	9	
14	15	16	
21	22	23	
28 Black Friday	29	30	

DECEMBER

2025

MONDAY	TUESDAY	WEDNESDAY	THURSDAY
1	2	3	4
8	9	10	11
15	16	17	18
22	23	24	25
29	30	31	

FRIDAY	SATURDAY	SUNDAY	NOTES
5	6	7	
12	13	14	
19	20	21	
26	27	28	

JANUARY
2026

MONDAY	TUESDAY	WEDNESDAY	THURSDAY
			1
5	6	7	8
12	13	14	15
19	20	21	22
26	27	28	29

FRIDAY	SATURDAY	SUNDAY	NOTES
2	3	4	
9	10	11	
16	17	18	
23	24	25	
30	31		

FEBRUARY
2026

MONDAY	TUESDAY	WEDNESDAY	THURSDAY
2	3	4	5
9	10	11	12
16	17	18	19
23	24	25	26

FRIDAY	SATURDAY	SUNDAY	NOTES
		1	
6	7	8	
13	14 Valentine's Day	15	
20	21	22	
27	28		

MARCH

2026

MONDAY	TUESDAY	WEDNESDAY	THURSDAY
2	3	4	5
9	10	11	12
16	17	18	19
23	24	25	26
30	31		

FRIDAY	SATURDAY	SUNDAY	NOTES
		1	
6	7	8	
13	14	15	
20	21	22	
27	28	29	

APRIL

2026

MONDAY	TUESDAY	WEDNESDAY	THURSDAY
		1	2
6	7	8	9
13	14	15	16
20	21	22	23
27	28	29	30

FRIDAY	SATURDAY	SUNDAY	NOTES
3	4	5	
		Easter Sunday	
10	11	12	
17	18	19	
24	25	26	

MAY
2026

MONDAY	TUESDAY	WEDNESDAY	THURSDAY
4	5	6	7
11	12	13	14
18	19	20	21
25	26	27	28

FRIDAY	SATURDAY	SUNDAY	NOTES
1	2	3	
8	9	10 Mother's Day	
15	16	17	
22	23	24	
29	30		

JUNE

2026

MONDAY	TUESDAY	WEDNESDAY	THURSDAY
1	2	3	4
8	9	10	11
15	16	17	18
22	23	24	25
29	30		

FRIDAY	SATURDAY	SUNDAY	NOTES
5	6	7	
12	13	14 Flag Day	
19 Juneteenth	20	21 Father's Day	
26	27	28	

JULY

2026

MONDAY	TUESDAY	WEDNESDAY	THURSDAY
		1	2
6	7	8	9
13	14	15	16
20	21	22	23
27	28	29	30

FRIDAY	SATURDAY	SUNDAY	NOTES
3	4 Independence Day	5	
10	11	12	
17	18	19	
24	25	26	
31			

AUGUST

2026

MONDAY	TUESDAY	WEDNESDAY	THURSDAY
3	4	5	6
10	11	12	13
17	18	19	20
24 31	25	26	27

FRIDAY	SATURDAY	SUNDAY	NOTES
	1	2	
7	8	9	
14	15	16	
21	22	23	
28	29	30	

SEPTEMBER

2026

MONDAY	TUESDAY	WEDNESDAY	THURSDAY
	1	2	3
7	8	9	10
14	15	16	17
21	22	23	24
28	29	30	

FRIDAY	SATURDAY	SUNDAY	NOTES
4	5	6	
11	12	13	
18	19	20	
25	26	27	

OCTOBER
2026

MONDAY	TUESDAY	WEDNESDAY	THURSDAY
			1
5	6	7	8
12	13	14	15
19	20	21	22
26	27	28	29

FRIDAY	SATURDAY	SUNDAY	NOTES
2	3	4	
9	10	11	
16	17	18	
23	24	25	
30	31		

NOVEMBER
2026

MONDAY	TUESDAY	WEDNESDAY	THURSDAY
2	3	4	5
9	10	11	12
16	17	18	19
23 30	24	25	26

FRIDAY	SATURDAY	SUNDAY	NOTES
		1	
6	7	8	
13	14	15	
20	21	22	
27	28	29	

DECEMBER
2026

MONDAY	TUESDAY	WEDNESDAY	THURSDAY
	1	2	3
7	8	9	10
14	15	16	17
21	22	23	24
28	29	30	31

FRIDAY	SATURDAY	SUNDAY	NOTES
4	5	6	
11	12	13	
18	19	20	
25	26	27	

Printed in the USA
CPSIA information can be obtained
at www.ICGtesting.com
CBHW082122081124
17118CB00014B/1742